Positive Thinking
How to be Positive by Eliminating Negativity

By David A. Hunter

Disclaimer:
The views expressed within this book are those of the author alone. The information contained within this book is based on the opinions, experiences, and observations of the author and is provided "AS-IS". No warranties of any kind are made. Neither the author nor publisher are engaged in rendering professional services of any kind. Neither the author nor publisher will assume liability or responsibility for any loss or damage related directly or indirectly to the information contained within this book.

The author has attempted to be as accurate as possible with the information contained within this book. Neither the author nor publisher will assume responsibility or liability for any errors, omissions, inconsistencies, or inaccuracies.

Table of Contents

Your Thoughts Can Eventually Make Or Break You

It was years before I truly understood and appreciated the power of my thoughts. I didn't believe that my thoughts would ever lead to anything even remotely significant.

Since I underestimated the power of the mind, I didn't see the point of positive thinking. I should also mention that things weren't exactly going well in my life.

Everything was the exact opposite of what I wanted it to be. I would get extremely frustrated when things went wrong. My frustration would lead to even more problems, making it difficult to break out of this cycle of negativity.

How do we break this cycle of negative events that leads us to more negative thoughts? How do we get out of this rut that we were thrown into against our will?

Many of us have a strong tendency to wait for our problems to go away all by themselves.

After we get tired of waiting for what feels like a lifetime, we begin to realize that time does not always take care of everything for us.

Thoughts are powerful, and once you steer your mind in the right direction, things can begin to get very exciting!

If you are experiencing a lot of problems at school, but your relationships, friendships, career, and health are in great shape, you might just need to change schools.

But when you are having a lot of problems with all of the above, your thought patterns are probably what really need to change.

Even the happiest people on the planet will still encounter some problems from time to time, but if you find yourself continuously being overwhelmed with trouble, there is good news.

Many of your problems can begin to fade away as you learn how to change your thinking patterns. The way you look at the world will become your world.

To put it another way, your thoughts will influence your actions, and then your actions will determine the events that happen throughout your entire life. I know how challenging it can be to think positive when there are so many things going wrong in your life, but until you change the way that you think, you will not achieve the life that you are looking for.

Since it's your life, you will have to take the initiative.

You can take control of your life, but you must take control of your thoughts first.

There are certain things in life that you can't always control, but it's time to start focusing on the things that you can control.

Not allowing your negative thoughts to control your actions is certainly something that you can control.

But instead of trying to directly weed out the negativity in your life, it's best to simply dwell in a positive state of mind.

Negativity is eliminated by acknowledging it and by choosing a positive attitude over it. Just like a parasite cannot survive in a healthy environment, negativity cannot survive very long in a positive environment.

By turning your mind into a solid foundation of positive thoughts, the negative thoughts will suffocate.

<u>Thoughts Mean Very Little Until They Turn into Emotions</u>

Your emotions are the offspring of your thoughts.

The reason that thoughts are so powerful is because you can't experience emotions without them.

That's why it's so important to get into the habit of positive thinking.

With enough persistence, your thoughts will begin to shape your reality.

The good news is that negative thoughts don't have to influence you unless you choose to dwell on them.

Thoughts are just the *conscious* mind doing its job, but emotions can give you actual insight into your *un*conscious mind.

It won't be enough to simply repeat over and over to yourself, "I am so happy," when you know that you feel upset about something.

It usually backfires by suppressing the bad emotions.

The idea is to avoid these chronically upsetting situations by thinking positive, and then by feeling positive.

If you lose a game when you are playing sports, it wouldn't make sense to tell yourself that you won when you know that you lost.

It *would,* however, make sense to try to figure out *why* you lost.

If you figure out what went wrong, you can begin to work on finding a solution.

After you find a solution, you can do better at the next game.

Before you can find out why you aren't experiencing enough peace and joy in your life, you must first be honest with yourself by acknowledging the internal dialogue that runs through your unconscious mind.

If you read a ton of scary stories one night, while saying to yourself, "I am at peace", you probably wouldn't feel very relaxed. This is because thinking about peace isn't enough.

You have to experience peace, but you won't feel calm until you get rid of the thoughts and emotions that are blocking your sense of calmness.

So, negative thinkers are basically watching horror movies in their minds all the time.

They want to be more positive, but they won't stop doing the negative things that sabotage them.

Positive thinking should not be confused with suppressing your emotions.

Your emotions are a reflection of your thoughts, and if you want your negative thoughts to change, you will need to change the way in which you react to negative situations.

You need to figure out why there are so many negative situations in your life.

Others might have been responsible for placing you in bad situations, but they aren't the ones who are responsible for keeping you there.

Encountering a negative situation that was not your fault does not mean that you have to turn yourself into a negative person.

Thoughts are very important, but much of the time, they must be converted into emotions if they are going to have any kind of influence over you.

It only takes a second to change your thoughts, but it can take considerably longer to change the way in which you actually feel about something.

If you are not used to thinking in a positive way, bad news will be more likely to leave a long-lasting negative impact on you.

You can't just wait until the last minute before you start to think in a positive way in hope of helping yourself out of a negative situation. It would be like waiting until after you are severely dehydrated before you finally start to drink water.

The more of a habit you make out of positive thinking, the more likely you are to experience the joyful emotions that lead to a genuinely positive life.

This means that if you want the positive changes in your life to be more than just temporary, you will need to let go of grudges, move on from the past, and break free from the things that are holding you back.

Negativity can make it very difficult to believe that everything will be alright.

It will be much easier to think positive when there is not a lot of negativity to hold you back, and once you are able to get into the habit of truly believing in your positive thoughts, your emotions will follow.

With that said, we also must be careful to NOT become overly reliant on emotions, as they can in fact be misleading.

Doing the right thing, for instance, will not always bring such great feelings, at least not in the short-term.

It's important that we do not allow ourselves to become manipulated through emotions, since they can be used against us.

But if we can focus on the good results that can be achieved in the long run, we can alleviate our emotions, even when the short-term task at hand is difficult.

For example, let's say a person has a goal of building a house.

But since that person doesn't have the money to do so, he must work hard and save lots of money to produce the income to allow him to turn his vision into a reality.

Working so hard and making other sacrifices might not always feel great in the short-term.

But by keeping the long-term goal in mind, this person can begin to experience a sense of contentment while he labors.

If this person had listened to his initial negative emotions that accompanied his distaste for such laborious work and cutting down on his spending, he never would have had a chance of achieving his goal.

We have to focus on the big picture, and even if we can't see the results of our own personal labors clearly at the moment, we must trust that they are there, one way or another.

It might not always turn out the way we expect, but we can at least use it as a valuable lesson learned when something doesn't quite workout.

How To Prevent Negative Thoughts From Turning Into Negative Emotions

So, if our thoughts can influence our emotions, how can we prevent our negative thoughts from turning into negative emotions?

No matter how much you practice positive thinking, negative thoughts will still work their way into your mind from time to time.

That's just the way it is.

Positive thinking is not about preventing negative thoughts from entering your mind, it's about preventing negative thoughts from controlling your life.

Refusing to acknowledge your negative thoughts will not help you when you are trying to eliminate negativity.

You eliminate negativity by dealing with your negative thoughts, not by pretending that they don't exist.

It's similar to dusting furniture. You can't stop dust from existing. You can't banish it from the earth. You just have to clean off the dust that has formed on your furniture before it builds up too much, and after you do that, the furniture can really begin to shine.

Positive thinking is something you need to keep up, otherwise, it will surely fade away.

Dealing with negative thoughts is not so much about applying one large, groundbreaking technique, as much as it is about applying a series of smaller techniques regularly.

In other words, it's not rocket science, but being consistent is key.

One way of dealing with your negative thoughts is to get creative with them. A house usually has more than one escape route.

There is usually a front door in the living room, a door in the back of the house, and a door in the basement that leads to the backyard.

Many people get into the habit of going through the same door day after day. When you encounter a negative situation, there is usually more than one way of looking at it.

If you aren't able to be flexible enough to expand your options, you could find yourself trapped inside of a very negative situation. Expanding your creativity will open your eyes to things that you were not able to see before.

Let's say that a store runs out of an item that you were looking for.

Instead of feeling depressed, you can think of it as an opportunity to try something new. Who knows?

You might end up liking the new item even better, and if not, you can think of it as a learning experience. You can't be certain about what you really like unless you are certain about what you dislike.

I know what it's like to think that you have found the perfect item.

You assume that there is no point in trying anything else once you have found something that you really like. That is a big mistake.

There are plenty of different things out there that might end up serving you even better, and it's important to keep an open mind about new opportunities.

You have the power to change negative situations by having a positive attitude combined with creativity. Whenever you encounter negative situations, try to find an alternate escape route. With enough creativity, negative situations can be turned around in your favor.

Comfort Zones Are Not As Comfortable As They Look

Staying within your comfort zone can make you feel like a more positive person, but this positive feeling is usually only temporary.

You might find it easier to block out negativity when you stay inside of your comfort zone, but by doing so, you will not be able to grow.

After you realize that you're not growing, your positive thoughts will turn into negative thoughts.

The things that are worth doing are usually the same things that require us to step outside of our comfort zones.

Refusing to step outside of your comfort zone can keep you stuck in a state of negativity in the long-term. Similar to physical fitness, you have to keep working on your ability to think positive.

By regularly challenging yourself, you will be less likely to fall back into old habits. Leaving your comfort zone can feel extremely unsettling initially, but it gives you much more back in return. It's kind of like taking 1 step back in order to take a couple of steps forward.

Even when you feel that you already have everything figured out, there always seems to be something else to learn.

It's the same thing with positive thinking. Even if you feel that everything in your life is going well, negative thinking patterns can sink back in.

It's similar to wearing braces. After the braces have corrected a patient's teeth, a retainer is required to make sure that their teeth do not go back to the way that they used to be.

Stepping outside of your comfort zone does not have to be overwhelming. Taking one small step at a time is fine.

Let's say that social gatherings make you feel extremely uneasy. It would be easier for you to stay in a positive mood if you just didn't go to an upcoming party, but never leaving your house can have a serious negative impact on you in the long-term.

This is when it would make sense to go to a friend's house where there will be just a small gathering of people that you know.

You could also go to a nearby park or a store. The idea is to challenge yourself without overwhelming yourself.

Facing any worries that you might have is a part of positive thinking. You need to have a positive outlook on everything. Negative thoughts can multiply as you continue to avoid the things that you dread.

It's about releasing yourself from your own personal prison. You don't have to befriend your enemies, but you will need to forgive them.

You don't have to do all of the things that you absolutely hate doing, but you will need to get over your fear of doing them. You don't have to always succeed at everything, but you will need to get over your fear of failure.

Let's say that you really hate math. You are worried that the teacher might ask you to solve a math problem in front of the entire class. In this case, stepping outside of your comfort zone would involve working on a math problem in front of the class. You wouldn't have to become a mathematician, you would just need to get over your fear of failure by stepping outside of your comfort zone. It would be difficult to stay in a positive state of mind if you were always worried about your math class.

If you don't get over your fear of failure, it can plague you in other areas of your life. The fear can overflow into the rest of your daily activities. Positive thinking is about happiness, but it's also about eliminating negativity by stepping outside of your comfort zone.

How To Use Expectation To Your Advantage

Depending on how you use it, expectation can bring you both negative and positive thoughts. If your expectations are too high, you might suffer from disappointment.

If your expectations are too low, you might not have the motivation that is needed to reach your fullest potential.

The first step is to expect good things to happen in your life.

Expecting bad things to happen can put you in a negative state of mind automatically. Even when you have to do some things that you don't want to do, try to look at the bright side. How can good things happen in your life when you don't even believe that they are capable of happening?

The next step is to be realistic about your positive expectations.

Since disappointments can be discouraging, you have to stop placing so much emphasis on short-term results.

People don't necessarily experience discouragement because their expectations are too high.

Many people experience discouragement because they are too focused on the short-term results.

It's alright to dream and think big, but you must first understand what it is that you really need.

You also have to understand that these things require patience. Just because something is taking a long time to happen, that doesn't mean that it can't happen, or that it won't ever happen.

I used to believe that being positive, and being realistic were two different things. Having a hard life turned me into a pessimist.

There were just so many things going wrong. It can take some time to break out of that cycle of pessimism, but as soon as I started seeing my problems as only temporary, I was able to make the transition to positive thinking.

Expecting all of your problems to disappear all by themselves is unrealistic. But expecting many of your problems to gradually fade away as you fix them is another story.

Positive expectation comes from believing that you are worthy of great things, and realistic expectation comes from the belief that if you work hard enough at your goals, you can achieve them.

Expect good things, work hard, and be patient.

Desires can be very go leaders.

They tend to lead us into the things that we need to do the most. After all, how can important things happen in our lives if we have no desire to make them happen?

How To Get Past Your Self-Critical Thoughts

When it comes down to your own mind, you are the one who has the most control over it.

When it comes down to your own thoughts, you are the one who has the most power over them.

When it comes down to criticism, many of us are often our own worst enemy.

Oftentimes, we hold ourselves back more than anything or anyone else ever could. Negative events might happen all around us, but we don't have to react to them in a negative way.

As long as you aren't putting too much pressure on yourself, there's nothing wrong with pushing yourself to move forward when you feel like you need a motivational boost.

But when we are continuously choosing to not believe in ourselves, continuously giving up before we even give ourselves a chance, and continuously beating ourselves up, we begin to slip into the category of being overly self-critical.

Many of us tend to believe that being extra mean to ourselves will help us to achieve our goals faster.

The more pressure we feel, the more tense we get, and the more tense we get, the more strict we get with ourselves. We don't want to give ourselves any breaks when we feel like we are falling behind.

We need to alleviate the pressure if we want the self-critical thoughts to stop.

Since you can't control others, you can't alleviate the pressure that they are trying to put on you, but you can alleviate the pressure that you are putting on yourself.

The pressure that is placed on us from external factors, is usually nothing compared to the pressure that we place on ourselves.

We might deal with our share of rude opinions from others, but that's not real pressure. The real pressure starts when we take those rude opinions, and then run with them.

It takes self-confidence to gain the courage to move on after you learn from your mistakes.

Self-criticism might lower your chances of making mistakes, but that's only because it usually keeps you from trying altogether. Our self-critical thoughts can easily turn into self-defeating thoughts, and our self-defeating thoughts can make us want to give up.

You can overcome your self-critical thoughts by realizing that they are not facts. Whether it's criticism from yourself or from others, you need to remember that the criticism is based on opinions, not facts. Criticism is usually based on only one part of a particular story.

Let's say that you want to get some chores done. You have a whole wardrobe of really expensive clothes that are nicer than anyone could imagine. Since you don't want to risk ruining any of your nice outfits, you decide to take some of your oldest, cheapest clothes to do your chores in. Someone walks by and sees you in your cheap outfit, and then they start to make comments about how you have "no idea" how to dress. They don't realize that they are the ones who have no idea what they are doing by making such a statement. If only they knew that as soon as you are finished with your chores, you have a whole wardrobe full of nice clothes waiting for you. There is a time and place for everything, and wearing a very nice outfit is hardly appropriate for doing housework.

When we are being self-critical, we often do the same sort of thing to ourselves. We just don't see the whole picture. We judge ourselves based only on the negative situation that we are currently in.

When you are in a negative situation, you need to think about all of the good things that you've done before, and all of the good things that you will do in the future.

Self-critical thoughts come from judging ourselves based on one side of the story. You need to stop taking a small negative thing and turning it into a large thing that takes up your whole life.

Self-critical thoughts are just opinions based on one side of the story, and that one side of the story is usually false anyway. They are lies, half-truths, and exaggerations.

Continue to remind yourself of that, and your self-critical thoughts will begin to vanish.

<u>There is Power in The Benefit of a Doubt</u>

Giving someone the benefit of a doubt will require you to not take things so personally, even when you feel like you are being attacked in some way.

You still acknowledge whatever it was that happened, but you decide not to make such a huge deal out of it.

Some people don't like to give anyone the benefit of a doubt. They like to assume the worst, and by doing so, they end up bringing out the absolute worst in themselves and others.

When we choose to give others the benefit of a doubt, we benefit from it more than they do. By giving others the benefit of a doubt, we decrease our own feelings of paranoia. A lot of our negative thoughts are the result of believing things that simply aren't true.

When you are unsure about whether or not something negative is true, for your own sake, it makes sense to assume that it's not true. You have nothing to lose, because even if it does turn out to be true, it won't help if you turn yourself into a negative person.

Don't be one of those people that overreacts when someone else makes a small mistake. The world already has enough of those people.

You need to give yourself a fair chance by giving others a fair chance. If someone went around spreading false rumors about you without any proof, wouldn't you want the people to give you a chance to tell your side of the story?

Let's say that you are putting up a house for sale. It's a perfect house that's worth $2,000,000, but since you have more than enough money to live off of for the rest of your life, you decide to put the house on the market for $250,000. Since you priced the house so low, people begin to think that there is something wrong with it. In this case, your generosity comes with a high price. You try to help people, but they end up avoiding you. They end up missing out on something really incredible because they did not give the seller the benefit of a doubt. They didn't have to commit to anything. They didn't have to buy the house. They only had to stop by to look at the house, but they wouldn't even do that.

You don't have to commit to anything when you give others the benefit of a doubt.

You need to become less reliant on the opinions of others, and more reliant on your own instincts.

If you feel like acting on a good opportunity when it presents itself, don't allow negative feedback to influence your decisions. Allow your instincts to guide you.

As long as there are no dangerous risks involved, giving others the benefit of a doubt can be very beneficial for you.

Sometimes we take things the wrong way, but even when something negative is being directed at you, it's better not to go jumping to conclusions.

Just because something negative happened, it doesn't mean that it was your fault.

Different things happen for different reasons, and you are not always responsible for what is happening around you. But you are responsible for handling your own thoughts before they take full control of you in a negative way.

Instead of worrying about what is happening in the outside world, concentrate on what is happening inside of your own mind. You are not the outside world. You are what your mind is, and your mind is who you are.

Try not to get so defensive when you are being falsely accused of something. Have the confidence to not let bad things get to you. The opinions of others don't have to have a negative effect on you unless you allow them to. But the opinions you have of yourself will effect you in some way no matter what you do.

The ability to give yourself and others the benefit of a doubt will show that you are very secure in yourself and comfortable with who you are. Insecurity is very negative, so we want to avoid that emotion.

Try to be understanding by looking at things from the other person's point of view.

Don't be one of those people who always complains without ever looking at the other side of the story.

They complain about the green side when they are on the blue side, and then they complain about the blue side when they are on the green side.

They have been on both sides of the story, but they always claim that the wrong side is whichever side they are not currently on.

If you are uncertain about who is right or wrong, it makes sense to stay in a positive state of mind. Being a cynic can be useful in a life or death situation.

No one likes to be taken advantage of, but we oftentimes overdo it with our inability to trust ourselves. We treat ourselves and everyone around us like criminals.

To illustrate, if a cashier hands out the wrong change, many people will assume that it was done on purpose. They might assume that the cashier was trying to pocket the customer's money. In this case, you should notify the cashier that they did not give you the correct change, but you should also realize that the cashier probably did not intend to give you the wrong amount of change.

Accidents happen and mistakes are made, but staying calm and positive is what will allow you to get through negative situations without making things worse.

Many people don't seem to understand that their negative thoughts are responsible for many of the negative situations that they experience.

Positive thinking will naturally lead to giving yourself and others the benefit of a doubt more often, but you can also use the benefit of a doubt to help you become a more positive thinker.

Either way works fine.

<u>How To Regain Control By Not Blaming Others For Your Problems</u>

Defensiveness seems to be a survival mechanism that many people use. Not a lot of people like to admit to being responsible for something bad happening.

Shifting the blame onto others seems to be an automatic reaction that many people have. The question is, *Why?*

Well, admitting that we were wrong about something means that we will also be obligated to fix the problem. A lot of people don't like the idea of having to take action to correct their problems.

What we fail to realize is that we give our power away each time we refuse to admit that something was at least partially our fault.

Victims are prone to powerlessness, and you won't have control over your life unless you have power over your mind. Victims are also more likely to drown in depression and hopelessness. Since they feel like something was taken from them by someone else, victims have a tendency to hold grudges. Instead of seeking self-improvement, they spend a lot of their time and energy on thinking about revenge.

It's time to reconsider your perspective. By readjusting your mindset, you can see things in a whole new way. Remember, you can only make yourself look bad. Saying something like, "You made me look bad", is really just your ego talking.

Bad situations are only as bad as you make them appear to be.

People can spread false rumors about you, but anyone that accepts those lies as facts probably isn't someone you want in your life anyway.

In fact, it can be a good test to see who your real friends are. A close friend will usually refuse to believe anything slanderous that was said about any of their friends.

Intelligent people should be able to decipher the truth from the lies, so why blame a gossiper for "making you look bad?"

Instead of worrying about what others are doing wrong, focus on doing the right thing for yourself. The right thing is to enjoy life by not taking it so seriously all the time.

The best form of "revenge" is to live a happy, healthy, and successful life. Karma usually provides enough justice. There is no need to feel like you need to get back at somebody.

I know it's difficult, but staying calm under upsetting situations has worked wonders for me over the years. Your thinking becomes much more clear as you allow your mind to reason things out. Instead of assuming the worst, and then sorting everything out later, it's better to stay calm in order to sort things out now.

I used to have a really bad, high-stress job. The negative environment caused me to jump to conclusions and assume the worst all the time. Since so many horrible things were always happening, it was nearly impossible to break out of that negative mindset. Years went by before I realized that the only person keeping me there was myself.

We are not responsible for the actions and behaviors of extremely negative people, but we are responsible for what we choose to tolerate.

Personally, it took me years to find a better job, but I could have tried so much harder to seek something better a lot sooner. It was a while before I had even bothered to look for something better because I didn't believe in myself. Once I regained my confidence, I found something much better. The better job wasn't hiding from me; I just didn't see the better job because I wasn't looking hard enough. I wasn't looking hard enough because I didn't believe that I had the power to to make the right decisions in my own life.

But we do have that power.

We have more power than we give ourselves credit for. A better life is waiting for you, but you need to believe in yourself in order to realize it.

Don't blame yourself, but don't blame others.

Blaming yourself for negative situations will lower your self-esteem, while blaming others will send your mind the signal that you are not in control of your own life.

Think of good feelings as a reward for thinking the right thoughts. Your mind is trying to let you know that you are heading in the right direction.

Continuously blaming yourself or others for things that are going wrong rarely leads to good feelings. It just causes more feelings of bitter resentment.

Treat complaining like poison, and avoid it. Treat the ability to have control over your own life like gold, and pursue it.

How To Tell The Difference Between Negative Situations And Exaggeration

Some situations in life are truly negative, but many of them are widely exaggerated. As emotional human beings, we tend to overlook the logical part of our circumstances.

If you're not careful, you can get carried away in a sea of overwhelming emotions. So, is the negative situation you are going through really that bad?

Sometimes a negative situation is really not negative at all. We interpret things a certain way based on how we are thinking.

Let's say that it's springtime. There is one person who likes cold weather, and then there is another person who likes hot weather. Both of these people might dislike springtime because one of them thinks it's too hot, while the other person thinks it's too cold. If both of these people realized that springtime is sort of a combination of summer and winter, they would be able to change their thinking patterns. The person who likes hot weather can rest assured that it's not wintertime, while the person who likes cold weather can be thankful that it's not summertime. These are two different people with totally different preferences for the weather, but they are still able to enjoy the same season.

Sometimes the weather starts to heat up, and then we start to assume that we are about to begin a long, hot summer.

We lose our jobs, and then we automatically assume that we will never see money again.

We go through traumatic experiences, and then we assume that we will never recover.

We get stuck in abusive relationships because we don't believe that we can do any better.

We go along with the crowd because we assume that following our dreams is less important than being miserable.

Exaggeration can really become a bad habit that branches off into many different areas of your life.

Put your emotions aside for long enough to allow you to see the situation for what it really is.

Fear and insecurity can cause you to feel like your negative situations are the end of the world.

Believing in yourself can allow you to realize that your negative situations are just there to remind you that much better times are up ahead.

How To Battle Through Negative Experiences, And Then Turn Them Into Positive Ones

Negative experiences present themselves in many different shapes and forms, but the thing they all have in common is that they all seem to take away our ability to experience good emotions.

Even as a positive thinker, negative situations can still present themselves in your life without much warning.

But did you know that every negative experience we go through can actually make us stronger?

The reason that some people don't get any stronger after enduring negative situations is because they refuse to learn from them.

They prefer not to make mistakes at all because they don't know how to learn from them. If we go through a negative experience, we need to make the best of it.

You can't expect to win a game if you are just going to stand on the sidelines the whole time.

Why do we always assume that an uncomfortable experience has to turn into a living nightmare? I believe that a fear of change combined with a fear of uncertainty are what lead us into this type of thinking. We don't trust ourselves to handle the situation, even though we are actually quite capable of doing so.

As long as we are willing to learn and improve, we can handle almost anything. Negative situations are like stepping stones to reach positive experiences. Just like you have to work hard in the gym to get fitness results, you have to battle through your negative experiences in order to reach positive ones.

Negative situations are your chance to practice being thankful for your opportunity to learn from them.

To illustrate, picture retaking a test that you previously failed before. Instead of seeing it as more work to do, you can see it as an opportunity to improve your grade.

Negative situations are opportunities to improve our lives. We just need to take a look at what we did wrong, and then find a solution to the problem. We need to stop seeing unexpected changes as opportunities for destruction, and start seeing them as opportunities for positive growth.

Once you find out what you did wrong, the negative situation already begins to shift into a more positive one. If the color yellow has caused you to get sick, that could just be a friendly warning that red is actually the right color for you. If yellow was the wrong color for you, it would be much worse if you did not get sick. You never would have known that a much better color was out there for you.

Instead of pursuing something better, we have a tendency to try to force something to happen that simply is not right for us. Certain situations will feel negative, but it's always for a reason. We have to think about what's causing the negative situation to be so negative, and then we need to step into the right direction.

Think of it as a game of "Hot or Cold." If you took a step in the wrong direction, the person would tell you that you were "getting colder." This wasn't to insult you. The person was just trying to steer you in the right direction.

Negative situations can be turned into positive ones as long as we allow them to steer us in the right direction.

Even if you lose something or someone important, you can use that as a chance to be thankful for what you do have. Sometimes we can't see how many good things we really have until a negative situation serves as a wake up call.

Once you understand that negative situations exist to serve a purpose, you won't even see them as negative situations at all, but as building blocks to becoming a stronger person.

Thanks for reading.

More from David A. Hunter

Self-Esteem: Know Your Worth by Building Self-Esteem, available at all *Amazon* stores, including <u>U.S.</u>

How to Find Happiness, available at all *Amazon* stores, including <u>U.S.</u>

How to Deal with Anger, available at all *Amazon* stores, including <u>U.S.</u>